YOLT

you only live twice

Junior

Cindi Jasa

YOLT Junior

For publishing inquiries, contact:
YOLT Publishing
c/o CMI
13518 L Street
Omaha, NE 68137

ISBN: 978-0-9982931-3-4

Publishing and production services by Concierge Marketing Inc.

Library of Congress and Cataloging-in-Publication
data on file with the publisher

Printed in the USA
10 9 8 7 6 5 4 3 2

I want to dedicate this book
to my grandchildren Emily, Evlyn,
Zeke, Xander, Bri and Brynn.

For Eliza, Ethan and Caleb, I look
forward to passing this book on to
your children one day.

I love each one of you more than
you will ever know!!

Has anyone ever told you that children are VERY special to God? When Jesus came to earth, He loved to spend time with children. It made Him very sad when people tried to keep the children from Him.

Do you also know that God loves to talk to children? I think that's because lots of grownups are too busy to listen when God talks to them so He talks to kids like you.

If you have never heard God speak, that doesn't mean He isn't talking to you. It may just mean that

you don't know how to listen for Him or know what His voice sounds like. Sometimes He may put an idea in your head, or He might use someone else to tell you what He is thinking.

I do know one thing that God wants you to know. HE LOVES YOU VERY MUCH!! And His love for you doesn't depend on what you do or whether or not you love Him back. He will always love you!

When God created you, He had special things He wanted you to do. You may think you have to wait until you are grown up to do things for God but that isn't true. If God is helping you, you can do big things for Him and for other people right now - no matter what age you are.

Have you ever felt like you weren't special or that no one loved you? If so, maybe you don't know how God feels about you. He was so excited when He created you!! Before you were even born, He knew all about you and about the person you would grow up to be.

You weren't just born into a family. God put you there. He chose who your parents, brothers and sisters would be. He put you in the family you are in for a very special purpose. You may or may not like where you are, but God doesn't make any mistakes, so that means this is the perfect place for you.

Life can be hard sometimes but God is always there to help you. If you don't know who God is, then you probably don't know that you can ask Him for help.

If you have a problem that is really hard for you and you don't know what to do, talk to God about it. He REALLY cares about everything that happens to you and He has the best answer for your situation. He wants you to learn now, while you are young, to ask for His help. Then when you are grown up, you will already know how to do this.

Many children ask for lots of things because they think that toys, clothes or games can make them happy. They don't think they can really be happy unless they have everything they want. Then kids grow up to be adults and want bigger things. They are still looking for ways to be happy.

God says you don't need a lot to be really happy. He says you only need one thing. That one thing is Jesus.

Have you ever played with a toy which has shapes that you have to put into the correct holes? I bet you didn't know that you have a 'hole' in your heart where only God can fit. Just like the toy, you have to choose what to put in the hole that is in your heart.

If you choose things other than God to make you happy, your heart will have an empty spot because Jesus is the only One who can fill it.

Are you thankful for all that God has given you? Think about all the good things in your life: your family, your friends, food, and a house where you can live. Those are just a few things. I bet you can think of a lot more!

Instead of only thinking and talking about the bad things which happen in your day, what if you start thinking and talking about all the good things?

God loves it when we stop to say 'Thank You' to Him (I'm pretty sure your parents like it when you thank them too!).

When you are upset or bored, try telling someone what makes you happy. You can even make a game of it. This will put a smile on your face and you will be happy again.

Have you ever heard the story about how much Jesus loves you? Before you and I were born, God knew we would do things that would make Him sad and could keep us out of heaven. Because He loves you, He made a plan so that wouldn't have to happen.

He asked His Son, Jesus, to come to earth as a baby and live with us. He never did anything wrong. He always obeyed his parents and He loved people all the time. He was even nice to people who were really mean to Him.

Then the people who didn't love Jesus decided they wanted to kill Him. They didn't know that was already part of God's plan. So they hung Him on a cross to die. Jesus still loved and forgave those people.

Have your parents ever punished you for something you did? When Jesus died on the cross, He took the punishment for every bad thing you would ever do. Your parents still need to correct you but God forgives you for those things. He looks at your heart.

It hurts God's heart when you aren't nice to someone, tell a lie, get angry, want your own way, talk badly about other kids or say mean things. But you can ask Him to forgive you because Jesus died for those wrong things He knew you would do. God also says that if you want Him to forgive you, you have to forgive other people.

God uses people you may think are mean to teach you how to be kind. Sometimes they might just need a friend. You could make a big difference in their lives just by being nice to them. You might be the only one who is kind, but do it anyway.

There are different ways that God speaks to you - one way is by reading the Bible. Have you ever gotten a letter from someone who told you how much they love you? That's what God's Word (the Bible) does. It lets you know how much God cares about and loves you.

Another way that God talks to you is in prayer. You might think that you don't know how to pray very well, but that's not true. Prayer is just talking to God like you would talk to your best friend. It's not about asking God to give you lots of things that you think will make you happy. It's more about asking God what will make Him happy.

God wants to be your best friend. He loves it when you talk to Him all day long. He always hears your prayers even when it doesn't seem like He is listening.

Praying isn't just about talking to God. It's about listening to Him talk to you. When you get together with your friends, does one of you do all the talking or do you take turns? God wants to take turns with you. Sometimes He wants to talk while you listen. You can't hear Him speaking if you don't take time to listen.

God gave me a friend who is from Zimbabwe, Africa. She lives in the United States now, but God wants her to help the people in her country who don't have much. He told me to help her do this. Because we heard God, lots of people were helped and a village worked together to build 4 bathrooms for their church. Other people were given food to eat. We also want to build a house for their pastor.

Then God told us to collect shoes for the children in Kenya, Africa. They have to walk to school and many of them don't even have shoes. It's very hot there and it's hard on their feet. They also have little bugs called "jiggers" that get in their feet. Their feet get so sore they can't go to school.

Instead of birthday gifts, we asked our family and friends to donate shoes for the children. We want to take shoes to children in four schools in Kenya (about 500 children). We also want to buy things to help children who already have the jiggers so their feet can get better.

So far, we have collected over 500 pairs of shoes to bring to Kenya. God knows everything we need and how many children don't have shoes, so we are asking Him to send us all the supplies that they need.

We are going to take the shoes to Kenya and pass them out to the children in the schools. It will be quite an adventure!

God loves YOUR prayers. Your prayers make a difference in your life and in other peoples' lives. God loves it when you talk to Him about everything!

God doesn't always ask us to do big things like take shoes to Africa, but if He puts an idea in your head, He wants you to let Him show you what to do with that idea. It may seem too big for someone your age, but if God gives you the dream, He has everything you need to help you do it. He loves it when we listen, but He really loves it when we obey Him.

Do you know that God isn't mad at you? He smiles when He looks at you. He loves it when you tell Him that you love Him. I do think it makes Him sad when you say His name in a bad way, but when

you thank Him for all the good things in your life, it makes Him really happy.

Did you know you can't be good enough to go to heaven? Jesus was the only one who never did anything wrong. Some people think that if they do enough good things, that will get them in to heaven. But there's only one thing you need to do.

Jesus wants us to be part of His family. You have the family that God placed you in right now, but God's family lasts forever. Jesus died so you could be part of His family. But getting into His family is a little different than being born into one. It's called being 'born again'.

To be a part of God's family you need to ask. You can do that by praying a prayer something like this:

"Dear God, I want to be a part of Your family. Thank You for sending Jesus to die for me. I accept Your gift and I ask you to make me Your child. I want to live my life for you. Help me to hear You when You speak to me. But more than that, I want to obey what you tell me to do. Give me a thankful heart. Thank you for my family and everything You have given me. I love you Jesus. Amen."

If you prayed that prayer, welcome to God's family!! Someday soon, Jesus is coming back to earth to take everyone who loves Him to live with Him forever. I'm excited for that!

While you are waiting, you need to remember that everything you do in this life makes a difference in the next life (heaven). God has gifts for people who listen and obey Him. If you live your life to make God smile, He will make you happy too, even when sad things happen to you.

And remember that HE ALWAYS LOVES YOU!! Follow the big dreams God gives you and watch how He uses YOU to change the world!!

More books by YOLT Publishing

Choices—*Every choice you make has a part in shaping your life for good or for bad. With that in mind, you may want to consider the decisions you make on a daily basis. Ultimately the choices are up to you, so I urge you to choose wisely!*

The Power of a Dream—*This story is about how God brought two totally different people together to change a little piece of the world.*

YOLT: You Only Live Twice—*Have you ever considered that everything you do in this first life has an eternal impact on the second life? You only live twice so it's wise to think about what you are living for. There's too much at stake to live life without purpose.*

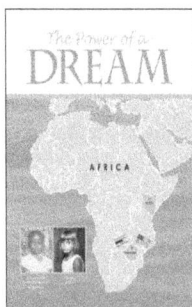

www.YOLTPublishing.com